nectar
WORDS OF SELF-LOVE & CARE
Derek R. King & Julie L. Kusma

Nectar
Words of Self Love & Care

ISBN: 9798352348024
ebook available

"Kintsugi (金継ぎ, "golden joinery"), also known as kintsukuroi (金繕い, "golden repair"), is the Japanese art of repairing broken pottery by mending the areas of breakage with lacquer dusted or mixed with powdered gold, silver, or platinum, a method similar to the maki-e technique. As a philosophy, it treats breakage and repair as part of the history of an object, rather than something to disguise."

https://en.wikipedia.org/wiki/Kintsugi

"Wabi-sabi (侘寂) is a world view centered on the acceptance of transience and imperfection. The aesthetic is sometimes described as one of appreciating beauty that is "imperfect, impermanent, and incomplete" in nature. It is a concept derived from the Buddhist teaching of the three marks of existence (三法印, sanbōin), specifically impermanence (無常, mujō), suffering (苦, ku) and emptiness or absence of self-nature (空, kū)."

https://en.wikipedia.org/wiki/Wabi-sabi

together
we are magic-
we are the keys
that unlock
each other's
soul

Derek & Julie

Treasured
is the metal gold
but not as much to me
as my precious soul.

Love
yourself
for there is
no other
thing to feel.
There is
no other
emotion
that is real.

Let go
of all worries.
Resign to the fact
the Universe knows best.

It's time to forgive myself
and forevermore
simply
BE.

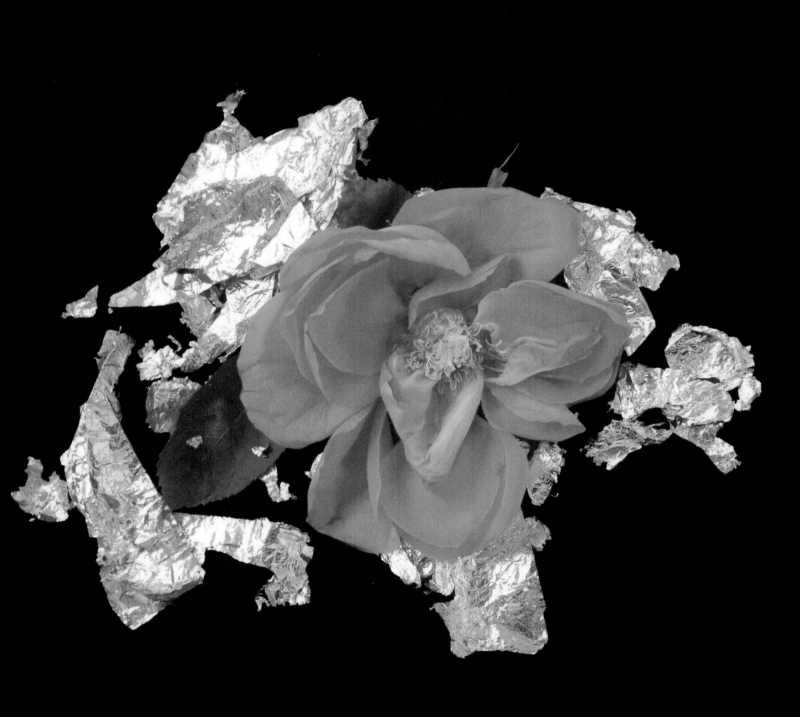

Let your uniqueness glisten.

The sun shines bright
in honey glow.
Upon us, its gifts
it bestows.
Of light and magic
and healing growth,
it restores us and
makes us whole.

In the sweet divine
I shall simply rest
healed and restored.
In this place called love,
I am truly blessed.

Seek
the gold
within
your
heart.

I release
this garment
that hides my soul
and make room
for my heart
to grow
and glow.

Your
natural
beauty
is as
good
as gold.

Our
whispered
words
in loving
hues
bond us
together
as one
we fuse.

The
essence
of life
is simply
to be kind.

I closed
my eyes
& allowed
heavenly gold
to pour over me.

Restore
the calm
with
goodness
and
sweet
words.
Replenish
your true self.

**Feel
the force
of the light Divine
forever & until
the end of time.**

The places
I allowed life
to break me
weren't visible
so, I filled myself
with love's
golden rays
& let light
shine through.

A honeycomb
of sweet
golden words,
let them flow
into your soul.

I am authentically golden.

Take care
of delicate
you.

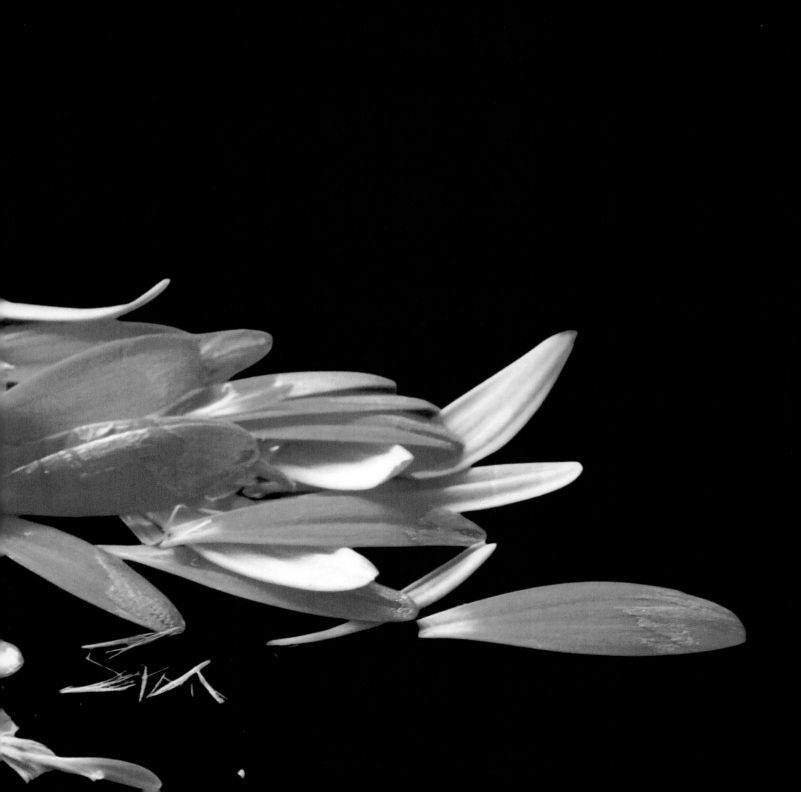

You
are always
You.

Choose you.

Heal and mend.
Raise your spirit.
Be true.

When you love yourself everything is gold.

Guild
every part
of yourself
with golden love.

**Our healing words
to our wounds
do tend.**

When
I care for me,
I care for you.

When you love yourself-
you allow yourself
to glow.

We are healed
by loving words
flowing into our souls.
Now, we are perfectly
imperfect.

Within your beauty is.

You are divine.

Be at one with yourself.

Self-love
is the nectar
that nourishes &
heals the soul.

Golden are
the loving words
which heal and mend.

Like a flower's petals,
every part of me
deserves love.

Embrace
the you
you're meant
to be.

Make time to care for all of you.

Rejoice in splendour
and let new life begin.

A lifetime
of scars upon
my skin
begin to heal–
restore my body,
& renew my mind.

This golden glow,
created by light,
fills your souls
with pure delight.

Derek R. King & Julie L. Kusma

our collaborations

Children's' Concept Books
What Might You Get? 26 Gifts of the Alphabet
Alphabites: the Alphabet One Bite at a Time

Children's Storybooks & Picture Books
The Enchanted Winter Faerie Realm (MG & YA Fantasy Poetry)
Jaggy Little Babies (Bedtime Story)
The Poetry Mouse (Inspirational Storybook)
The Enchanted Faerie Realm (MG & YA Fantasy Poetry)

Educational Books
Our Planets: Moons, Myths, & More
Our Trees: Botanics, Beliefs, & More

Inspirational Books
Moonrise to Moonset and All the Stars In Between (Love Poetry)
Sunrise to Sunset and All the Hours in Between (Love Affirmations)
Holoi 'ikepili; Words to Release & Cleanse (Ho'oponopono Affirmations)
Buddha's Garden: Allowing & Non Attachment Haiku
with love, the Universe (YA & Children's Philosophy Affirmations)
Honey: Words to Heal & Mend (Kintsugi Inspired Affirmations)

Keepsake Books
Our Halloween: Mysteries, Monster, & More
Our Christmas: Traditions, Memories, & More (Family Holiday Keepsake)

The Lighter Half Series
Alpha, The Lighter Half, Volume 2(Cosmology Poetry)
Amore, The Lighter Half, Volume 2 (Love Poetry)
Abracadabra, The Lighter Half, Volume 1 (Gaia Magic Poetry)

The Darker Half Series
Unchaste, Volume 11 (Erotic Poetry)
Santa's Claws, Volume 12 (Gothic Holiday Poetry)
The Darker Half, Volume 13 (Gothic Poetry)

Derek R. King

Derek R. King is a poet, musician, and the award-winning author of Noir (or When the Night Comes), Natyre Boy, and Honey: Words to Heal & Mend with his co-author Julie L. Kusma.

He lives in Scotland, where he enjoys the great outdoors, long walks in the hills, the sounds of the seas and ocean, art, and photography.

His published work:

More Red Roses in Verse (Love Poetry)
Urban (Environmental-Nature Poetry)
(the) Elegy (Book 3 in Poetry Trilogy)
Twelve Red Roses in Verse (Love Poetry)
Natyre Boy (Book 2 in Poetry Trilogy)
Noir [Or, When the Night Comes] (Book 1 in Poetry Trilogy)
The Life and Times of Clyde Kennard (Nonfiction Historical Biography)

For more of Derek's work, visit http://DerekRKing.uk
Follow him on Twitter https://twitter.com/DerekRKing2
TikTok at https://tiktok.com/@derekrking2

Julie L. Kusma

Julie L. Kusma is a multigenre, award-winning author who currently lives in the United States where she pens speculative fiction short stories, children's books, inspirational, educational, and novels. She holds a Master of Science in Health Education and a Master of Art in English, Creative Writing, Fiction.

Her published work:

Knock at the Door: An Inspirational Oracle (YA)
Squeak! (Children's Picture Book)
The Crooked Crone & Other Mystifications (YA *Supernatural Romance*)
Which Witch Are You? An Inspirational Halloween Oracle (YA)
The Circus is in Town (*Children's Picture Book*)
Eggie's Easter Counting & Color Fun with Jill Yoder
(*Children's Picture Book*)
Where Wildflowers Grow (*Children's Picture Book*)
That's Creepy, Santa! The Trilogy (*Holiday Horror*)
A Perfect Place for Scary Monsters to Hide with Jill Yoder
(*Children's Picture Book*)
The Many Worlds of Mr. A. Skouandy (*Psychological Horror*)
Pigglety Pigglety Poo (*Children's Picture Book*)
Stuck That Way & Other Quandaries (*Paranormal Horror*)

For more of Julie's work, visit http://julie-kusma.com,
Follow her on Twitter at https://twitter.com/juliekusma,
TikTok at https://tiktok.com/@juliekusma, and subscribe on
YouTube at http://youtube.com/c/juliekusmaauthor